GOLF: Energy in Motion

It's not about the ball;
It's about possibilities!

by

Debbie Crews Ketterling, Ph.D.

Acknowledgments

This book honors many! First and foremost I would like to honor my dad, Bob Lindsay, who introduced me to the great game of golf. This man loved the game, was a student of the game, and he was also a GREAT performer of the game. He guided me to my teacher of the game, Manuel de la Torre, who I have respected since I met him at the age of 13 years. Manuel had a knowledge of the physics and mental side of the game that far surpassed his time. Of course I would like to honor my mom, Meryl Lindsay, who drove me to the golf course endless trips, who plays very well herself, and who is a model of how to :"be" when we reach our 80s. My brother, Don, and my sister, Jane, have always supported me and my endeavors and I would like to "Thank" them.

I would like to honor my husband, Corky Ketterling, who helped me create this book and who designed all the illustrations. More importantly, his love and support are greatly appreciated. Corky helps me be who I want to be. My children (Danny, Armando, Keisa, Cameron, and Alissa) have taught me many GREAT lessons on how to live life. And of course, my animals (30+) who know how to live in the present, adapt, love, and care!

Lastly, there are the many golfers and non-golfers that have allowed me to observe, teach, consult, and test them over the years. Their lessons are throughout this book in many forms. I would especially like to honor Gaelle Truet for her contributions to this book and to life.

I have always believed that the great questions in research come from the real world, and these people have provided both the questions and the answers!

THANK YOU !

Table of Contents

Golf: Energy in Motion

Introduction

This book is written to enlighten golfers to perform what we want, when we want it, on the golf course. It is about performance, an integral part of learning and playing this great game of golf. In order to perform it is necessary to achieve a synchronized state of being that allows those great shots to flow through the system (mind, brain, and body). The "system" itself is a remarkable entity that is available to assist us in whatever we want to accomplish. It is more often the case that the performer is unclear, undecided, and possibly in a state of being that interferes with the system's performance. Learning to work with the system and to continually observe and adapt is the challenge of the game. It provides us with many exciting possibilities everyday that we play. If we choose to accept these challenges, the possible outcomes are tremendous. They are often greater than we could imagine. Believing in this concept of endless possibilities from which we choose, prepare, and perform is the first step to enhancing performance. Once we choose to believe, the energy starts moving in the desired direction.

Energy is the base of everything we do. Everything is made up of energy and thus, how we choose to direct the energy determines the outcome, the performance. Thus, energy

Golf: Energy in Motion

in motion is about synchronizing many sources of energy through motion to achieve the desired outcome. Our goal is to facilitate the transfer of energy throughout the motion. The euphoria we feel when this happens, I believe, is why we play the game.

The fascinating part is that we have choices. We can choose to have the energy work for us or against us. Energy is always in motion so we can direct it however we choose. And if we don't choose, someone or something else will probably choose for us. But in reality, this simply means that we are choosing not to choose.

Energy flows in patterns at various levels of performance. For us to be able to define these patterns is important for us to be able to change the patterns. Then, if we choose to change the patterns, it will require energy to create new paths to optimal performance.

Key Concepts

Thirteen Key Concepts

There are 13 key concepts that provide a framework for experiencing "energy in motion" golf. We will go through them one at a time. The order of achieving these concepts is different for each golfer. Therefore, I will put them in a logical order for your reading; however, each golfer will need to decide for them self. There will be some repetition of the important points within each concept. "Intensity" is a key variable that will run through each of the 13 concepts. ENJOY!

1. The Game of the Game

2. Awareness

3. Intention

4. Attention

5. Create GREAT Golf

6. Optimize the Filter

7. Sink-chronize for Success

8. Adaptability

9. Choices

10. I Know

11. Control the Dial

12. Magic Box

13. Believe

Golf: Energy in Motion

Getting on the Same Page!

There are several terms that need to be defined before we start. They may not be universally agreed upon definitions; however, they will be common ground for this reading.

Learning is defined as "a relatively permanent change in the skills and ability to perform a task, a result of experience" (Schmidt, 1988). This does not mean that because we "know" what it is we want to do, that we can "do it". It means that a high percent of the time we are successful at achieving our goal (relatively permanent). It also implies that to be learned it is experienced. This means that if the motion is performed correctly at least one time, a motor program has been established to create the desired outcome. In research, a skill is considered learned if it has retention and transfer. If 70% of the time in the field (our field is the golf course) it can be repeated after time has passed (one or two days, minimum) and it can be transferred to a slightly different task, (different club, different target) it is considered learned. (It requires an 80% success rate in the laboratory.)

Performance is "how a task is executed (created) at a given point in time" (Thomas & Thomas, 1994). Every shot in golf is created, not executed and certainly not repeated. This concept will be discussed in more detail in Chapter 5. How motion is completed at each moment in time is the focus of our intention and attention. These are the precursors of successful performance.

State of Being refers to our physical, psychological, emotional, and intuitive self at a given point in time. It is transitory and is controlled by the performer. However, on occasion, that little white ball thinks it controls our state of being and on occasion, certain golfers give that little white ball all the control. This can change!

Sending refers to a state in which our focus of attention is on transmitting information (efferent signals) to the muscles. It is more commonly referred to as "making it happen." Sending occurs primarily during the learning process and on the range.

Receiving is a state in which our focus of attention is on the information returning from the muscles (afferent signals) more commonly known as feedback. It is a "let it happen" frame of mind and is a necessary state for the golf course.

Mind is the "director." Mind was first defined by Descarte (early 1600s) as our awareness, our consciousness, and he believed the mind exists outside the body (Hawkins, 2002). Descarte coined the phrase "I think, therefore, I am."

Golf: Energy in Motion

Intention is simply "what do you want?" Energy follows intention; therefore; it is very important to carefully and specifically define our intention.

Attention is defined as a psychophysiological state of directed energy. How we focus our thoughts will either facilitate or inhibit performance. Also, we either direct our thoughts and attention the way we choose to, or they will be directed for us by outside variables (distractions, etc.).

Energy is vitality, intensity, vigor, power, the ability to do work.

Arousal is simply a state of increased activation in the system. It is a necessary component to focus our attention.

Intensity is the amount of energy transmitted, the degree of energy.

Anxiety is arousal with a negative label on it. Arousal in-and-of-itself is not bad, it is only when we label it as "bad" or "interference" that it becomes anxiety. We have a choice!

Balance is when opposite sides of the system balance each other. Thus, if activity is high on the right side of the brain in a defined area, it will also be high on the exact opposite side of the brain in the same area. Balance in the system helps create physical, mental, and emotional stability.

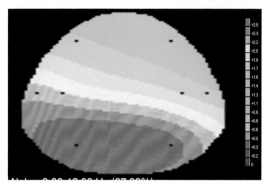

Balance Between Right and Left Electrodes

Reading Brain Maps

1. The picture is viewed from the top of the head down.

2. The dots represent the electrode locations.

Synchrony refers to various components of the system vibrating together. Synchrony is a higher level of synergy in which the system is not trying to balance itself, it is simply functioning as a unit.

3. Brighter color = more activity in the brain location.

4. The frequencies are theta (top left), alpha (top right), beta (bottom left) and beta2 (bottom right).

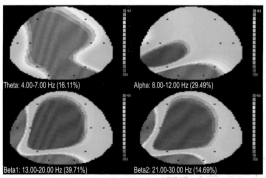

Theta: 4.00-7.00 Hz (16.11%)   Alpha: 8.00-12.00 Hz (29.49%)

Beta1: 13.00-20.00 Hz (39.71%)   Beta2: 21.00-30.00 Hz (14.69%)

5. The goal is for all four frequency bands to look similar in color.

6. Similarity is more important than the amount of activity.

The two bottom maps are synchronous but not the two top maps.

Golf: Energy in Motion

Harmony is a combination of parts in the system performing as a pleasing and orderly whole. This includes agreement in feeling, action, ideas, interaction and attention. It is as if a director (the mind) from outside the system is creating order and does so by being both the instigator and observer at the same time. The ultimate state for optimal performance is a state of harmony in the system. This can be achieved, and the process of achieving this state is explained in the remainder of this book.

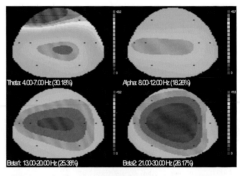

Novice Golfers—Non-Harmonic

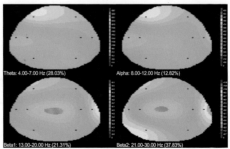

Elite Golfers—Harmonic (4 similar maps)

The System refers to the mind, brain, and the body. The interrelationship of these three entities is described below:

Mind   Intuition
              The Director

Brain   Thought, Sending, Receiving
              A Recording Device

Body   Emotion, Feeling, Sensing
              The Actor

This book contains science boxes (purple boxes) for those who like to read the data behind the scenes There are "key" concepts in the margins to emphasize important points. Lastly, there is a Story Window at the end of each chapter. They are true stories. ENJOY!

Golf: Energy in Motion

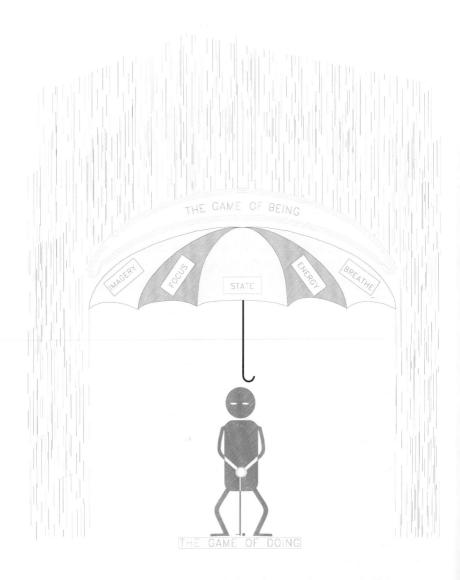

The Game of the Game

What we are "doing" on the golf course is playing the game of golf. Who we are "being" while we play the game of golf I will refer to as the "game" of the game of golf. Who we choose to "be", on any given day, at any given point in time, will determine our performance. It is imperative that we also play the "game of the game" if we want to score. The game of the game is that which surrounds the game of golf. While we are on the golf course we "do" activities that pertain to golf approximately 2 hrs total.

Golf Total Time

4 hrs of play, shooting 75

Hitting the Ball	2 s X 75 = 2.5 min
Preshot Routine	20 s X 75 = 25 min
Preparation	30 s X 75 = 37.5 min
Socialize	15 s X 75 = 18.75 min
Caddy	30 s X 75 = 37.5 min
Total	121.25 min (~2 hrs)

We then have 2-3 hrs to "be" someone who is either going to facilitate or disrupt our performance. We have the choice!

Golf: Energy in Motion

So how do we decide who we want to be on a given day? Often, a large percentage of who we "be" is determined subconsciously or automatically. It has been estimated that we may spend as much as 70% of our day in automatic (Bargh & Chartrand, 1999). If this is true, then we participate in the round of golf more like a conditioned robot than like a performer who regulates their state for optimal performance. Many golfers believe that we want to perform in an automatic state and that is somewhat correct. But we don't want to play the whole 4-5 hours in an unconscious state unless we are in the zone (the zone being a unique exception). If we are unconscious, we will simply fall into all of our old patterns and it will be unlikely that we will have an optimal experience. Furthermore, what is automatic? And once we get to automatic, do we stay there? Clearly we know that some days are more automatic than others. Singer, Lidor, & Cauraugh (1993) described five different stages of automatic. I often find experienced, high skill players become too automatic and we need to reel their consciousness back in the game.

The Game of the Game

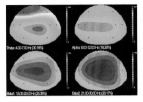

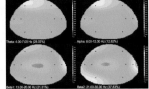

Novice Golfers   **Expert Golfers**

The optimal state for performance is actually a state of heightened consciousness or heightened awareness. If we look at the recordings in the brain we see that expert performers (brain map on right) actually have increased activity compared to novice performers (brain map on left) or new golfers. In addition, the brain maps indicate that a state of harmony exists in the brain when golfers perform well. This is indicated by the consistency of color across all areas of the brain and across all frequencies in the power spectrum analysis.

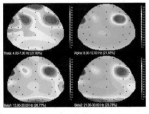

What is fascinating is that even beginning golfers who achieve an optimal state for play have brain patterns that are similar to elite golfers. While their performance

Novice Optimal State

may not be at the level of elite performers, their state will facilitate their performance.

Those who do not participate in the game of the game, or who play from their head,

Golf: Energy in Motion

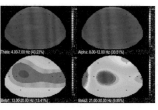

typically have increased left hemisphere activity and disruptive performance. The left hemisphere is primarily responsible for analytical, logical thinking, it is sequential, verbal, and sees things in parts. The right hemisphere is our creative, imaginative, thinking side. Timing, rhythm, balance, and automatic performance are more a function of the right side. The left hemisphere is very important as we prepare to hit the ball, but it must finish its job. **The most consistent finding from all sports is that the left hemisphere must quiet in the seconds preceding the motion.** In golf, the right becomes slightly more active as we prepare to move and this is what helps create the state of harmony in the brain (Crews & Landers, 1993).

Playing from our brain is like playing from a recording device, and this does not lead to best performance. In fact, I believe that players who are playing from their head are playing nowhere near their capacity. Playing from our body is not enough either, although it may be better than our head. Ultimately, we want to play from the integration of both the head and the body, and the director/ integrator is the mind.

Under pressure situations it is imperative to play from our mind. Our thoughts and feelings are likely to be unbalanced, but our mind has the ability to synchronize our energy and perform at a very high level.

Story Window

I have had the good fortune of discussing performance with two great performers—Alan Alda and Geena Davis. Alan Alda was able to create his "acting state" to putt, and he performed his best in this familiar state. He achieved this state by jumping up and down and by using a stationary bike to increase his heart rate. Alan also uses the audience to get himself "up" for acting. He claims that it helps him focus.

Geena Davis competes in target archery to take a break from acting. However, when she wasn't scoring well at the National Archery Championship, she imaged being one of the best female archers on the team, and her performance improved. We can all "be" whoever we want to be in our mind, and it will affect our performance.

Golf: Energy in Motion

Awareness

Awareness is the second key to energy in motion golf. If we are not aware, we cannot influence our performance or make change. Once we become aware we can go through a process that will put us in control and provide the opportunity to create whatever it is that we choose. Optimal performance is actually a state of heightened awareness. This implies that there are levels of awareness and that it is at higher levels that we perform best. The key is getting to these high levels. Increased activity in the brain that is harmonic in nature, reduced tension in our body, and increased intuitiveness create this state.

We become aware by simply asking for it. If we put our attention on our routine, we will know what we are doing, and we will know if it changes. Anything we want to influence or change we simply focus our attention in that direction. If necessary, we evaluate it and become accountable. This will ensure that we are aware of it. Once we have achieved awareness, the second step is to "make it okay." However it is, is okay! It's simply a baseline or starting point for where we want to go. If we fight what we want to change, we will make it bigger because we are feeding it so much energy. This doesn't work! Once we make what we want to change "okay," we can

Golf: Energy in Motion

then make a decision about our direction. If we decide to change, then a plan must be put into place. Therefore, we have a four-step process:

1. Become aware

2. Make it okay

3. Make a decision

4. Plan a strategy

This can all be done in a few seconds of time. The result is clarity, intention, and attention that will lead to improved performance.

During a round of golf when all is well, we are already in a state of heightened awareness, and nothing needs to be done. Play and enjoy every minute of it. On days when we are not in this same great place, we can increase our awareness by "doing" (hitting shots) and then by stepping back and observing (observing what is happening). This may take place after each hole, after each shot, etc. So we switch off between being the "doer" and being the "observer."

Be the Observer!

All of this can only take place by playing in the moment! "Be" in the motion. It is not enough to simply "Do" the motion. We have many "Doers" in golf. They are the range hitters that scrape a ball over and hit it, scrape a ball over and hit it, etc. It is easy to fall into the pattern of doing instead of being.

It is only by being fully aware that we perform optimally. The subconscious is primarily responsible for creating the motion, but the conscious must be in a state that will facilitate this process. In other words, the conscious and subconscious must be on the same page. In heightened awareness we feel everything important, our perception of time slows down, we are very connected to the target, etc. This is a state of higher intensity, not relaxation. There is no tension in the body, but the brain is active and harmonic. Thus, intensity is important to achieve heightened awareness.

Observation has taught me two primary styles of play. One I would call "expressive" and the other one I would call "controlled." It is important to define our style of play because two quite different strategies are used to help these players perform. The expressive player has more variability in scoring (i.e., 65-80, 78-92, 100-120). The controlled player has a smaller range of scores (i.e., 68-72, 75-80, 95-100).

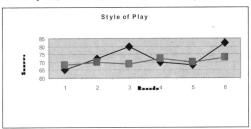

Expressive Player (Blue) - Controlled Player (Pink)

Golf: Energy in Motion

Both golfers are consistent in their own style of play and both golfers usually don't really want to play like the other style of player. They may think they do, but it does not fit their personality. They all say they want to be more consistent, but the truth of the matter is that they are consistent. Most golfers want to be consistently better!

The expressive player has no problem shooting the low scores, putting together a string of birdies, etc. They simply lose it on a hole or two and end up with double or triple bogeys. This golfer is the home run hitter that strikes out on occasion. The goal is to make the strike-outs base runs instead. The strategy to work with this golfer is to find out their tendencies on the high scoring holes and reduce or eliminate the double and triple bogeys (penalty shots, 3-putts, etc.).

The controlled player may not be as comfortable shooting low scores. They usually have a definitive comfort zone and if they start scoring low, they may subconsciously sabotage their play. It is more important to help this player be comfortable with low scoring. Adjusting the image they have of themselves as a golfer and teaching them to work with their intensity can be beneficial. State of mind coordinates with the style of play of the golfer. The continuum below defines four states of mind typically experienced on the golf course: aggressive, assertive, maintain and protect.

Mark a "G" on the line below indicating

SMART FIRST!

|——————————|——————————|——————————|

Aggressive   Assertive   Maintain   Protect

the state of mind when you are playing Great and a second mark "N" indicating when you are Not playing well. Typically golfers will be on the left end of the line when they are playing well. The expressive player will probably be more left than the controlled player. When golfers are not playing well, they will be on the right half of the line. It is very important to stay on the left half of the line to perform well in golf no matter which style of play you use. It is the assertive/aggressive state that creates good scores and if anything, golfers need to increase the intensity of their state of mind as they continue to play. The key is to always be smart first. If I am smart in choosing my club and my shot, this will allow me to swing aggressive/assertive. Smart always comes first!

Smart First then Aggressive/ Assertive

The last thing to consider in style of play is patterns of performance. Statistics will indicate if a player typically starts strong and then falls apart, puts them self behind the

Golf: Energy in Motion

eight ball and then rallies back, or simply loses focus during the middle holes. Once a pattern is defined it is possible to work with it. Performance will always be going up and down. It does not follow a straight line. Reducing the swings in the direction of higher scores and moving in the desired direction (lower scores) is important. If a pattern can be defined, it can be changed. Inconsistent patterns suggest that the outside world, or the story is running their game. The story is what is going on around them and is constantly dictating their play instead of the golfer simply completing the task at hand (hit the chosen shot!). They are reacting to every incident instead of responding to the conditions and playing their own game.

Allport has a model of personality that fits well for golfers (Feist, 1985). He believes in a core personality pattern from which people operate. Behaviors, perceptions and

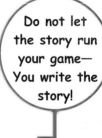

Do not let the story run your game— You write the story!

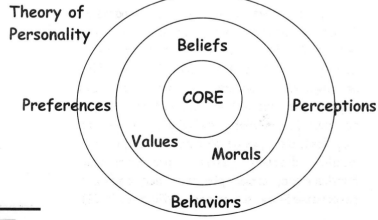

Theory of Personality

Beliefs

Preferences

CORE

Perceptions

Values

Morals

Behaviors

preferences can be changed quite easily to create changes in our lives. Morals, values, and beliefs are more stable, yet they may need to change over time for bigger life changes. It is our core personality that is stable and this is probably very important. This is who we really are, and who we really are is great! We simply need to know who this is so we can operate more effectively.

Theory of Motion

Timing

Positions   CORE   Preferences

Rhythm   Balance

Mechanics

I also   believe that people have a core movement pattern. Research shows that people have very consistent timing patterns in their hand-writing motion. (Schmidt, 1988). This would be an important concept for golf. It would suggest that people have motion that is unique to them (i.e., walking, swinging). Fast people play fast, slow people play slow. Changing this would disrupt their performance. Furthermore, under pressure our dominant response will always emerge (Williams, 2001).

So if we change a golfer's motion too drastically from their core movement pattern, it is not likely to hold up under pressure.

Appendix A contains a "Player Awareness Inventory" that demonstrates the connectedness between what we "do" and our "being." It is simple to answer the questions that pertain to you in a "Yes" or "No" response. Additional notes may be written when appropriate. Perhaps you will discover some insights into your "being."

Story Window

A Gateway Tour player who had previously been a hockey player, came for help with his game. He was definitely an expressive style player, trying to be a controlled player. When he realized it was okay to be an expressive player, to be himself, he started to score and enjoy the game again!

A Nationwide Tour player was struggling with his performance on the course (only). I asked him to put stars along the bottom of his score card for every swing he was able to "Feel the Finish" in the golf tournament. His initial round was 40%. This was his baseline and his awareness! The goal was to increase to 50%, 60%, etc. If we don't have awareness of what we do in competition, it will be difficult to change. Anything we choose to change, we monitor for awareness, and then we can observe the improvement.

Golf: Energy in Motion

ASK FOR WHAT YOU WANT !

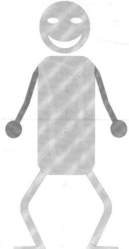

Intention

To "ask for what you want" sounds relatively simple. However, it is important to think very carefully about what it is that we <u>really</u> want. Do we want to make an awesome swing? Do we want to put the ball in the hole? Do we want both? It is okay to ask for what we want, all that we want. In fact, if we don't ask, we are probably likely to get less than what we want. The body wants a set of clear and specific instructions so it can create the outcome we want. The system's job is to create what we ask for, the best that it can, at this point in time. The instructions may be verbal, visual or feel. Now, if we doubt the system's ability to give us what we want, or we don't really want it (i.e., lay up short), the subconscious will jump in there and help us out. However, sometimes the subconscious overreacts a bit and interferes with performance.

> Ask for what you want! Clear, specific, instructions

For example, when we approach the tee and assess the situation, the brain receives and records everything it sees and knows about the situation. It pulls up from long-term memory everything related to this experience. Then, in accordance with what we are asking for, it creates a motor program. Once this is complete, the messages are sent to the muscles (efferent information), the brain receives feedback throughout the motion (afferent information) and continues to synchronize the motion (at a subconscious level) until the motion is complete. If the brain (conscious) stays in a neutral-to-positive place and doesn't interfere, the task will be performed quite well. If the brain contains negative thinking and self-doubt, it will influence the motion and the performance. Keeping the conscious in a good state of mind is critical to complete the task correctly. This is a "receiving" state of perceived control with excitement about where the ball is going!

I often find with skilled players, or with players who have progressed at a fast pace—they don't ask for enough. Their belief system is behind their skill development. They want more proof before they are willing to use their skill in meaningful play. However, it is only in meaningful play that we will receive the feedback to convince our perception that the skill level is real, consistent, and holds up in pressure situations.

Expectations are another variable that interfere with our intentions. They often come from the outside environment and then we internalize them. The good news is that if we take them in, we can send them away, and choose not to own them. It is important that we don't let the energy of expectation interfere with performance (Toole, 2004). Expectations either increase or decrease our intensity and often put us in a "try too hard " mode. As soon as we go to try mode, then we don't really believe! The language of expectation includes:

1. Have to
2. Need to
3. Should
4. Try

Words to Eliminate: Have to, Need to, Should, TRY

All of these words are banned from the golf course. They are worse than "four letter" words, and they are simply "not an option." My preference is to throw expectations out the window and simply ask for what we want!

The system is set up to give us what we ask for from both a psychological and physiological perspective. Goal setting is known to be the most effective psychological intervention to create change. From a motor control perspective, we have two systems that govern motion: the stimulus-response-system and goal-directed behavior. The stimulus response system is habit. We put in a stimulus and pair it with a response. This pairing becomes repetitive, automatic, or what we know as a habit. However, sometimes the response we are getting is not what we want. Therefore, if we want a different response we have to ask for it using a different stimulus (goal-directed behavior). This is how we change motion. We change the energy input system.

Don't complain about what you wish you are but embrace exactly what you are

Golf: Energy in Motion

Story Window

An LPGA teacher attending one of the LPGA Educational Seminars, was hitting on the range. She was small, but determined, and hit her favorite club very well. However, her 3 wood was not flying. When she walked up to her favorite club she was clear, committed and in charge, When she walked up to her 3 wood it was like someone else stepped into her shoes (meek, scared, etc.). Then she used the attitude of her favorite club with the 3 wood, and the shot improved. Her rating of the 3 wood shot was a "6" on a scale of 1-10 (10 is high). I asked her to hit a "7", she said "okay" and hit a "7." Then I asked her to hit an "8" and she said "okay" and hit an "8." I asked her to hit a "9" and then a "10" and she did both. What changed was her intention and performance followed! Interestingly, you get what you ask for!

Golf: Energy in Motion

Attention

How we focus our attention before, during, and after the swing directly influences performance. How we focus our attention between shots influences our ability to focus during the shot. This is actually our state of consciousness! We have a vast amount of attentional capacity in our brain. We either focus it the way we choose or it will be an open slate for negative thinking, self-doubt, and distractions.

There are many ways in which we can focus our attention in golf; however, they fall into two main categories. Category One is what we think about and Category Two is "how" we think about what we think. Of the two categories, how we think is much more important than what we think. What we think (i.e., swing cue) simply provides a window to help us achieve a state that will facilitate performance. How we think can be divided into:

> How we think is more important than what we think!

1. Internal or external

2. Broad or narrow

3. Sending or receiving

4. Active or passive

5. Intensity (level)

6. Informational or emotional

Golf: Energy in Motion

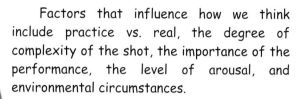

Factors that influence how we think include practice vs. real, the degree of complexity of the shot, the importance of the performance, the level of arousal, and environmental circumstances.

Internal or external and broad or narrow refer to the direction of focus. There are times when it is important to be externally focused in golf (i.e., the target) and times when we are more internally focused (i.e., feel). Our best performers in the laboratory typically tell us that they are focused on target, feel, or both when they are performing their best. It is possible to focus on both since we can parallel process (think of two things at once). The only requirement is that we prioritize our thoughts. On good days, target will probably be the primary focus and feel may be the secondary focus. When the motion becomes disrupted it may be important to focus on feel as the primary thought and target as secondary. In golf, the focus is broad as we approach the ball and becomes narrow as we get ready to move. For example, using a clock on the putting hole and seeing the ball roll in over a certain time on the clock can be very effective. It helps to program the system to create exactly what we want.

Sending and receiving provides a way to think about the direction of information/ energy exchange. The focus of attention can either be on the efferent message the brain is sending to the muscles or on the afferent information returning from the muscles to the brain. The focus can be on receiving information from the target, or on sending the ball on its way to the target. On the golf course it is important to be in a receiving state to gather information to then send the ball to the target. Thus, the focus would be on the information provided by the target and on the messages coming from the muscles if we want to score. This will evoke a "let it happen/ create" style of play instead of a "make it happen/force it" mode. On the range we may be in more of a sending mode to teach the muscles the desired motion. Novice players occupy most of their focus in a sending mode; however, they can still play in a receiving mode. The receiving mode allows us to self-correct during the motion at the subconscious level.

Active and passive focus can be described in the following example. If a friend picks us up from the airport and drives us to our hotel, we observe and enjoy the scenery. However, if we are told half way to the hotel that we will need to drive our self back to the airport, we pay attention very differently for the rest of the trip. Some golfers fall into the "sightseer" (passive) category most of the time. Others attend to every detail and lose the enjoyment of the game (over-active). There are times to be

Golf: Energy in Motion

passively focused and times to be actively focused to perform well. We clearly have markers to find our way, but we can also enjoy the scenery!

Intensity is one of the most important variables for successful performance. The degree or level of commitment, concentration, belief, strength, etc. are the factors that determine our intensity. We often hear of players "willing" the ball in the hole. I believe this refers to their high degree of intensity. It is energy directed through intention, focus of attention, and ultimately motion. It includes the energy we have regarding the target. Optimal performance is a result of our intensity of play. In tennis we have a first serve and a second serve. It is because we are given a second ball that we can hit the first

Play with your first serve!

serve with intensity. I believe that most golfers play golf with their second serve because we don't perceive that we have a second shot. However, we always have a second shot and often a third, fourth, and so on. I challenge golfers to play more golf with their first serve. If we did, we would have fewer total shots!

A brief conversation about relaxation may be appropriate at this time. In the early 1990s I conducted a study comparing four different training conditions and their influence on putting performance (Crews, Martin, Hart, & Piparo, 1991). The four conditions were EEG biofeedback, imagery, relaxation, and control (reading Reader's Digest magazines). The results indicated that EEG biofeedback and imagery were both beneficial to putting performance, while relaxation actually hurt their putting scores. The golfers were better off reading a magazine than doing relaxation exercises because they became too unfocused. Breathing is the strategy that I believe is most beneficial to create an intensity level that will facilitate performance. Many players hold their breath when they feel anxious and this is the worst option. Breathing "out" is an optimal way to start the routine, to let go and center before the motion, and to release after the motion. If players want to relax, it is a lot easier to simply watch golf on TV.

Focus of attention during a round can either be on information or emotion. We are constantly being bombarded by both. Feedback comes in both forms as well. Information is important for learning so we make good choices and the system can learn from the previous motion. Emotion is important because it is our source of energy.

Golf: Energy in Motion

E-motion is Energy In Motion

"E-motion" is "Energy in Motion." We need emotion to play; however, we don't want our emotions to run our game. Thus, separating information from emotion can be very helpful to focus our attention appropriately.

To assess a player's most appropriate level of intensity, I ask three questions:

1.   Are you good at hitting trouble shots?

2.   Do you play better or worse when you get angry (not frustrated)?

3.   Imagine a 6ft putt and rate your level of intense focus on a scale from 1-10 (10 is high) if the putt is for birdie___, for par_____, or for bogey_____. Then I ask, "Which putt do you make the most of?" This indicates their ideal level of intensity for putting, and probably for the rest of their game.

Trouble shots are interesting and often golfers who do better with higher intensity also play trouble shots well. On trouble shots we make good decisions, breathe, image the shot very clearly, walk up to it with meaning, hit it, and let go of expectations. We focus very well for this shot. It is the easy 7 iron in the middle of the fairway with no trouble around the green that becomes our difficult shot. It only becomes difficult because it does not demand higher focus. If we simply ask for more on the easy 7 iron, it too will require the appropriate level of focus and help create best performance.

> As we age, our focus of attention strategies may change. Molander and Backman (11989) have completed research indicating that heart rate patterns change in older, skilled miniature golfers. A small study we conducted in the 1990s showed that right and left hemisphere brain patterns also reversed among older, skilled performers compared with young, skilled putters (Crews, 1994). Their poor putts showed decreased activation in the final three seconds before the putt (see below).

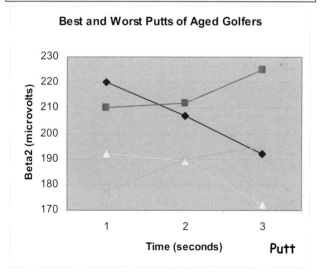

Best and Worst Putts of Aged Golfers

Best Putts: Right (Pink), Left (Aqua)
Poor Putts: Right (Blue), Left (Yellow)

Golf: Energy in Motion

Story Window

The tour players have such a fine sense of feel that one small change in their focus of attention can create awhile different swing. Michelle Estill, who has played on the LPGA Tour for 16 years, typically used "target" as her last thought before swinging the club. Performance wasn't going well, and she realized that her "target" stimulus was no longer working. She habituated to the stimulus, and it not longer created the increased energy state in her brain necessary to create the motion. She changed the thought to "hit the target" and bingo—the great shots were back! Her cue became internal, active, and intense. The response was the desired motor program, and performance improved.

Golf: Energy in Motion

Create GREAT Golf

O ne of the most important pieces of information I have learned from the laboratory is that every shot in golf is created. It is not repeated or executed! "This is the one and only time I have the opportunity to hit this shot, under these conditions, in this state of being." The task at hand is to put the pieces of the puzzle together, the best I can, to create what I want. If the goal is to repeat or even to execute, it does not imply increased intensity and in fact, intensity may go down. This will decrease our chance for great performance. No matter how good our practice swing is, it is possible to create an even better swing at the ball because it means more and has the ability to increase activation. More activity in the brain, and in particular, more right brain activity, allows us create shots we would never create in low, relaxed conditions. This is the fun of the game! Whatever we can imagine, we can create. In reverse of that, if we can't image it, we probably won't create it. Image refers to any form of seeing, hearing, feeling, sensing, or knowing!

Every shot in golf is created!

Creating great shots results from setting ourselves up the best we can, before and during the motion. Before the motion we decide and ask for what we want, very clearly and specifically. We breathe and imdge the

Golf: Energy in Motion

shot, usually from behind the ball. Then we aim. Arousal level and intensity must be set before we walk up to the ball. Emotions must be in a neutral-to-positive place before we are allowed to walk up to the ball. Once this is established, we walk up to the ball with meaning and set the club in place. As we complete the routine, we are focusing our attention to facilitate the motion we choose to create. The more creative we can be, the better. This initiates a state of mind that includes "watch this" and "I can't wait to see where this ball is going!" "Watch this!" is the best place we can be before we create the motion. It is a confident, powerful state of mind. Waiting to see where the ball is going reduces our need to control the ball! The small amount of unknown (where the ball is going) is part of the challenge that keeps us interested in the game. If we knew where every shot was going, we would be bored and probably take up another sport. There is a direct inverse relationship between the degree of unknown and the reward of hitting a GREAT shot. Enjoy the challenge!

Watch this! I can't wait to see where this ball is going!

Creating every shot has two primary components—start and finish. Science tells us the importance of starting and finishing each shot that we create (Proctor & Dutta, 1995).

1. The more complex the task, the longer the programming time. Longer programming time takes place behind the

ball. The motor program is created behind the ball.

2. Movement is coordinated relative to space and not to joints in the body. The mind, brain, and body plan the motion; the joint angles and muscle torques follow. If joint movements are used, they are only effective if all motions of all the joints involved are timed so they reach their <u>final</u> position at the same time, and then the motion is fluid. Focusing on moving the handle of the club through space, in the desired path, can be very effective. If the swing is finished in balance, facing the target, many components of the swing had to fall into place without having to focus on each one separately. <u>Finish</u> is the end of the swing—not impact. If the finish is correct, it is likely that impact will be correct since it is the bottom of the path.

Start and Finish!

3. Errors in motion can be detected before they are <u>physically</u> produced. They can be altered. Self-correction at a subconscious level takes place many times during the motion.

4. While hitting the ball with a bat, variability occurs in the time to initiate the swing, and not in the motions of the swing. Also, variability is in the <u>direction</u>

of the start, not at contact. In golf, the first three inches of the swing are critical, and they are easy to monitor and make correct.

5. Even when the two hands start a motion asynchronously, they tend to end in synchrony. The body is great at self-correction during the swing.

6. Self-correction in the swing can occur in 190 ms. The swing is 2,000 ms. That is at least <u>10.5 corrections per swing</u>, partially dependent on the speed of the club for the desired correction..

7. Goal-directed behavior suggests that if we know where we are going to "Finish," the body will get there in the most efficient, effective way possible.

Story Window

Michelle Estill was nonexempt for the 2004 LPGA season. She had been pumping gas in Wisconsin for extra money. The Corning Classic gave her an opportunity to play, so she came by Phoenix to get ready. Putting was okay, but the balls weren't dropping in the hole. Michelle decided to put some creative attitude into the routine. Before she hit every putt in the Corning Tournament, she said "Watch this, it's going in!" Michelle was leading the tournament after two days. She was one stroke ahead of Annika Sorenstam. Michelle finished tied for second behind Annika!

For three years I ran an attention deficit golf group. The four boys were 9-11 years old. For three years we used ABC: Aim, Balance, and Camera to hit each ball. Aim the club, balance the body, and end with a photo finish, smiling at the camera. The first day we went on the course (we only worked on the putting green and course), one player scored bogey, bogey, bogey, par in the 2 hrs it took us to play four holes. The ABC start and finish worked for everyone in the group for three years. If I attempted to add more cues to focus on, they performed worse!

FILTER BEing

Optimize the Filter

We are the Filter!

As we travel around 9 or 18 holes of golf, or more, it is our choice what we decide to let in for the day and what we choose to filter out of our round. We are the filter! We do not have to be a victim of the day. In other words, we do not have to attend to everything that comes into our head. We do not have to go up and down like a roller coaster to every event and outcome of performance. We have the option to change the channel and use only the information and events that contribute to successful performance. The rest of the information and emotion can be set aside (parked). Later, we can give the time and attention to the issues, and actually do something about them. It requires energy or activation in the brain to maintain the appropriate filters. Fatigue makes it very difficult to filter our thoughts and emotions. Therefore, obtaining an optimal state of arousal is the first step to filtering.

Schema Theory suggests that from a psychological and from a motor control perspective, we filter every piece of information that comes to us. From a psychological perspective, Schema Theory suggests that we have preset cognitions (thoughts) that influence input. Thus, if we go to a golf course and like the layout, if we have had good experiences there before, and if we

Golf: Energy in Motion

generally think positively about the course, we will interpret unlucky bounces differently from a course with the opposite set of preset cognitions. The good news is that we can choose our preset cognitions and thus, optimize the filter.

From a motor control perspective, Schmidt's Schema Theory (1975) suggests that generalized motor programs control motion (Proctor & Dutta, 1995). As a skill is practiced, the golfer learns the parameters necessary for the motion, and the system becomes faster and more accurate. Two schemas program motion. Recall schema programs in advance the initial parameters necessary to start the program. Recognition schema serves as a referent to compare incoming kinesthetic feedback. Fast movements are primarily governed by recall schema and slow movements use recognition schema to modify the motion during the performance. The back swing in golf is slow enough that we will self-correct. From the top of the backswing to impact is approximately 250 ms and there will not be time to adjust consciously unless the focus of attention is on a point past impact (Milton, 2003). The finish of the swing provides a focus point that allows for self-correction through the forward motion, even though the speed may be in excess of 100 mph.

When we are in the zone, we have an automatic filter in place that only allows input that contribute to my success today. The zone is a very special state that occurs when the conscious and the subconscious are completely coherent, and it is almost an unconscious state. It is likely to occur in meaningful situations when pressure may be elevated; thus, providing the extra arousal to be used for filtering.

Just below the zone is a conscious state we might call "optimal performance." This is a state in which we play great golf, but it does not happen quite as easily as when we are in the zone. Attention may need to be directed consciously to achieve the optimal arousal levels (thoughts that motivate) and then to focus on thoughts that stimulate the desired performance (image of the target).

One step below peak performance is "flow." Csikszentmihalyi's (1990) conscious flow state occurs when the demands of the task are slightly higher than our current skill level, and anxiety is low. Flow occurs often in everyday life if thoughts and emotions are synchronized with the task at hand. Flow occurs on the golf course for stretches of time when a positive pattern occurs. We can use a variety of techniques to get into flow, then move into peak performance, and on special occasions—the zone.

Golf: Energy in Motion

Practice contributes to optimizing the filter. There are two components to practice: a.) what we practice and b.) how we practice. Both contribute to our success. It is very important to vary practice, to carefully add challenge to our practice., and to have meaning in every aspect of our practice. We decide on our intentions and focus our attention to achieve what we want. At the end of the practice, we can clearly state what we accomplished and how we chose to spend our energy. My preference is to break down practice sessions into components (i.e., mechanics, rhythm, balance, routines, challenges, imagery, etc.). Fine tune the parts of the motion as a whole and then put them back together. Putting practice may include left-handed putts, right handed putts, eyes-closed putts, looking-at-the-hole putts, call-your-putt outcome (in, short right, long left, etc.) without looking at the ball roll, etc.

A brief conversation about practice swings may be helpful to optimize the filter. Practice swings must serve a purpose. Anything that we do that does not have meaning and serve a purpose becomes a distraction. Once we establish the purpose of the practice swing, then we determine where and when to use it. My preference is to keep them in a preparation routine rather than to include them in a preshot routine. This way we can use as many as we like. The information from the practice swing will be stored in short term/active memory until the next motion (the swing). For those players who are great practice swingers, but use a totally different swing on the ball, I suggest eliminating the practice swing. They don't need to practice it anymore, It is GREAT! It would be more valuable to think correctly over the ball.

Let's look at the intention and focus of attention during the full swing practice swing. Usually it is feel, rhythm, motion, etc. Seldom do golfers practice swing at full speed. Then when we take that 6 inch move to set up at the ball, the intention and the focus of attention often change. The focus becomes hitting the ball, get the ball to the target, etc. When the intention and the focus of attention are so different from the practice swing, why would we expect the practice swing motion to come out over the ball? If we eliminate the practice swing, we are more likely to focus our attention correctly over the ball and through the motion. There is no way we would "repeat" the practice swing when our intentions and attention are so different at the ball.

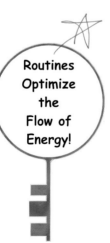

Routines Optimize the Flow of Energy!

Routines allow the system to relax and optimize the flow of energy through the system. When the body knows what is coming, and in the order that it is coming, it can run smoothly and stay at ease. If the system doesn't know what is coming next, it is always

Golf: Energy in Motion

Consistency before brings consistency during the swing!

on call to be ready for new information. Routines consolidate energy and provide confidence, perceived control, and consistency. Consistency before the swing brings consistency during the swing.

Fitness is important in golf to allow us to concentrate during the last three holes. As one's aerobic capacity increases, all of the daily tasks are completed at a lower percentage of our total capacity. Thus, we can perform physically and mentally more efficiently. Fatigue is one variable to avoid on the golf course. If we are fatigued we also have trouble thinking clearly and making good decisions.

We conducted a study (Piparo, Crews, & Hart, 1991) to assess fitness levels of golfers and found that fit golfers performed better following a 20 min walk at 80% of their maximal capacity, while unfit golfers performed worse.

Age is also an important contributor to performance. While age is associated with a decline in many of our physiological factors (i.e., strength, speed, flexibility), it offers us experience. This is a component that younger players may not possess. Experiences can work for or against us; it is up to us! Research indicates that older players maintain stroke consistency (Stelmach, Crews, Martin & Cheetham, 1998) and are still able to maintain performance. However, it appears that they may need to change their strategy to achieve the desired outcomes. They may not be able to do it the same way as when they were younger, but they can still score.

As previously presented in our discussion of attention, the brain patterns of four older players (ages 40-69 years) showed the opposite pattern of successful younger players. While activity in the brain decreases in the final three seconds prior to moving the club in younger players, it increased in the left hemisphere among the successful older players. The less successful older player trials showed a decrease in activity. This coincides with the work of Molander and Backman (1989) indicating that the heart rate patterns of older golfers increase as they prepare to putt compared to younger players who show a decreasing heart rate pattern. They also suggest that new strategies may be necessary to maintain optimal performance among older individuals.

Eat, drink and be merry! The last suggestion to optimize the filter is to take care of our physical and emotional needs on the golf course. Stay hydrated, eat to have energy to concentrate during the last three holes, and smile! All of emotion is expressed in the lower half of our face. If we smile we can transmit positive energy to our recording device in the brain. Optimize the filter!

Golf: Energy in Motion

> **Change the inside to change the outside.**

I have learned a great deal from working with the yips. If we change the outside (behaviors) without changing the inside (thoughts, emotions, beliefs, etc.), the positive effect won't last. The behavior improves temporarily—but the underlying pattern remains, and the yips will be back. I believe this is why the yips creep from putter to putter, from stroke to stroke, from putts to chips, etc.

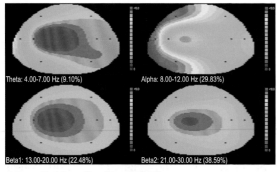

Yips Golfer (Left-Sided)

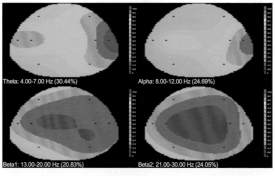

Yips Golfer in a Balanced State (Inside)

Story Window

Testing in the lab has provided many unique insights. When players optimize their filter and achieve a great state of mind, they perform unbelievably well. We attempt to disrupt performance by feeding tones in their ears, requiring them to push buttons on their putter handle while getting ready to putt, and by having them putt with eyes closed. For some players, no matter what we do to them they perform well, often better than their baseline-normal putting. It doesn't matter if they like the condition or not, or if they are comfortable or uncomfortable. They create an optimal energy state and perform better.

One Swedish European Tour player putt after riding 3 min on the stationary bicycle at moderate intensity. She made 10 out of 10, 13 ft putts on a putting green that never rolled the same for two putts in a row. These golfers optimize their filter, achieve a great energy state, and putt the ball in the hole!

SUCCESS

Sink-chronize for Success

Success, as defined by Merriam-Webster (1994), is "achievement of desired aim, something that turns out as planned or intended." This is very appropriate for golf. It suggests that we must decide on our intention, plan, and aim. While this definition is relatively straight forward, I'm not sure it happens like this on the golf course. The outside world has many of its own definitions of success (i.e., score, winning, placing, etc.). However, these definitions may only define success for a small portion of the people that play golf. Even for these people it may not be in their best interest to define success in the terms proposed by the external world. We have the option to define success from our own internal world that may serve us better!

There are many ways to define our own success on the golf course. It is not necessary to "win" a golf tournament to see myself as a "winner." In reverse, it may be important to see myself as a "winner" in order to "win" a golf tournament. This is defining success from the inside. Once we see our self as a winner, it is important to define what it will take to "be the winner." Score may or may not be a part of the equation. If score is included, my preference is to use a score range (74-79)

Golf: Energy in Motion

rather than a number. This gives us a little more latitude to perform.

Other internal definitions of success may include maintaining a specific state of mind or a thought focus for the round. While the goal is always to put the ball in the hole in as few strokes as possible, we must define the means by which we will achieve our goal. In addition, a "margin of success" for every shot allows us to set ourselves up to be <u>more</u> successful rather than to be unsuccessful. A margin of success (i.e., a 3 ft radius around the hole) allows us to feel good about ourselves even if the ball doesn't go in the hole. An example of this is when we choose to send the ball down the right side of the fairway and rule out the left side. We have probably defined a specific target, and we have now included a margin of success. There are "red light" zones (the left side), yellow light zones (the right side) and green light zones (the specific target area). Our body knows specifically what we are asking it to do! I would love to see more golfers do the same thing on the putting green.

To be successful on the putting green I believe it is important to "plan the miss" and "program the make." Unless the green is very undulating and fast, it would be beneficial to miss on the high side and long of the hole (within the length of the putter). This way the ball is moving toward the hole, and if we get a

<u>Plan</u> the miss and <u>Program</u> the make!

little tentative on the putt, it still has a chance to go in the hole. If we miss on the low side, the ball is moving away from the cup and picks up momentum from the break. This putt will end up farther from the hole due to the added momentum, unless we get tentative, and then it will be short of the hole or miss on the low side and not have a chance of dropping. So after we visually look at the grass behind the hole on the high side (planning), then we pick our spot around the target to put the ball in the hole (programming). The target spot is always done last so our intention is to put the ball in the hole.

People have fear of success and fear of failure, and I have yet to figure out the difference. Fear is fear and it runs the lives of many players. We can spend so much of our energy thinking about what we fear. If we simply spend less time thinking about it, it will have less control over us. Fear usually comes from the unknown. The extent that we can define our unknowns and instead focus on what we know we can do, is the extent that we can reduce and perhaps eliminate fear. We can set ourselves up for success.

FEAR:
False
Expectations
About
Reality

Choking is an example of successful play that becomes unsuccessful as a result of fear. The NBC "Dateline" study from 1997 gave us the opportunity to create a choking situation in the laboratory setting. Ten golfers

Golf: Energy in Motion

participated in the study and half of them choked while the other half were successful and earned $300 as a result of their putting success. The non-chokers resorted to similar past competitive experiences in which they were successful, focused on the task, and channeled their adrenaline into successful performance. The chokers became distracted, doubtful, and altered their routines (Anderson & Crews, 2001).

The yips in golf may be an extreme example of motion patterns evolving from fear. The uncontrollable spasm that occurs in putting, chipping, pitching, and even the full swing is more complicated than the golfing literature might suggest. There are clearly categories of yips-affected golfers. Some may be more psychologically disrupted and others appear to be more neurologically evolved (Smith, 2003). Fear and anxiety exacerbate the condition, but reducing fear and anxiety does not necessarily eliminate the problem. The treatment for each category of yips affected golfer is likely to be different.

Golfers often have trouble letting go of what we can't control (i.e., winning, bad lies, weather, etc.). It may be easier to look at these variables as "possibilities." Golf is actually a "game of possibilities," and the possibilities are endless. For example, on a windy day I believe we increase the possibility to win since there are many good players that

Golf is a game of possibilities!

don't perform well under these conditions. It may actually give more players a chance to win. No matter what is going on today, the possibilities of what can happen are always there. We have a choice to focus on what can go wrong or on what exciting challenge is in front of us. It is often this small piece of the unknown that keeps us going. (We still have a chance!) To transform fear and the unknown to a "game of possibilities" can lead us to our defined success.

Once we have defined success it is important to prioritize success. Do we want the ball in the hole or do we want to hit a great feeling shot? The one that is most important is the one we are most likely to achieve. Once the priorities are in order, we define the ladder to achieve the success very specifically and clearly. Every step on the ladder is important to achieve success and must be attained. Lastly, success in one area of our life must synchronize with other areas of our life. It is unrealistic to put in hours of practice weekly when we work a 50-hr week at a job (not golf) that pays our bills. It is also not necessary to put in hours on the range when we've played golf for a living the past 15 years of our lives. When we were young it was necessary to narrow our focus to become good in one area (golf). However, as we get older, if we want to perform well, it is more important to have balance in our life. There must be

Golf: Energy in Motion

synchrony and balance in our life in order to have synchrony and balance on the golf course and thus, to be successful.

Winning, as determined by the external world, is a goal over which we have less control. It is possible to play our best and not win and it is also possible to play marginally and win. In fact, most players who describe their best round ever, often say they were not even hitting the ball that good on the day they scored their lowest round. However, we can be a "winner" in many ways. We may not be the winner of the tournament, but in my book, if we have won once, we are defined as a winner. Depending upon how we define success, we may be a regular winner. The purpose of this discussion is to set ourselves up to be a winner and to be successful rather than to be unsuccessful. We never fail because we always learn. It is all perception.

FUN:
For
yo**U**
Now

Let's discuss having FUN. Success may be defined by how much fun we have playing the game. I don't know about you, but I don't have too much fun playing poorly. Playing well isn't always defined as fun either. Sometimes it is work, but we get the job done! I once had the opportunity to room with the Women's Olympic Gold Medal winner for rifle shooting and her description of the final day was "a tremendous amount of work that was not FUN!" However, she got the job done! I prefer to define fun as "**F**or yo**U** **N**ow!" This present experience is here at this point in time, solely for us to enjoy now. When we can totally "be" in the experience now, we have a chance of performing well and enjoying the outcome. Now that's FUN!

Those GREAT rounds we experience from time to time are there to let us know where we are going and what we are capable of performing. The goal after these GREAT rounds is to move towards these scores gradually and more consistently. We can do this by recording very specifically what we did to prepare for that GREAT round and what was unique on that day. This becomes our own personalized formula for success.

Story Window

One Arizona State University player who knew how to prepare for success used to find out the course record as soon as we arrived at a tournament. She had a definite routine to prepare to play, and stuck to it even if other players practiced more than she did. She played the course instead of the other teams.

Some of my favorite players are the 12-14 year olds. They play fearlessly because the hardware in their brain is not completely developed until the age of 15 years. They may struggle from 15-19 years old, but we can help them by teaching them to be analytical behind the ball and fearless over the ball. This way they sink-chronize for success!

Golf: Energy in Motion

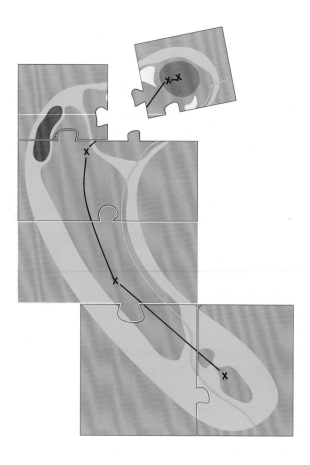

Adaptability

We are an oscillating system in an oscillating environment. Everything is always changing and it always will be. One of the most important beliefs for us to have about our game is that we are adaptable. No matter what the course throws at me today, I can adapt! I can play! It doesn't matter who I play with, how strong the wind is blowing, what "so and so" just said, or how many holes I am behind - I can play! Instead of taking my well practiced, structured, planned game and attempting to "fit it" to the course of the day, the goal is to take in (receive) from the course and play with the information and emotion that comes. It is our ability to put the pieces of the puzzle together the best way possible today that will allow me to enjoy the day and score. Practice and planning are important, but they are preparation for putting the pieces of the puzzle together in the most effective efficient way possible to play well and score.

I am adaptable!

One way that may be easier to put the pieces of the puzzle together is to work backwards. If we start at the end, "What do I want to accomplish today?" - or when I walk off the course, "What do I want to say about the day?" - then the words I choose contribute to how I plan the day. When I look at a hole and see where the pin is, see where I

Golf: Energy in Motion

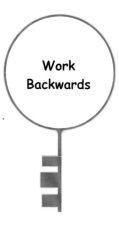

Work Backwards

Start and finish every shot!

want to come into the pin from, and work backwards to the tee, the hole lays itself out for me. When I swing the club and see where I finish the swing, that finish is determined by everything I did previously. If I finish where I choose, in balance, facing my target with all my energy expended, it was likely to be a very good shot (an 8, 9, or 10 on a scale of 1-10)! Working backwards allows the path to be defined by the end point. Otherwise I have to start from scratch and find all the pieces of the puzzle, put them together in a logical progression, and "hope" they accomplish my goal.

Adaptability also refers to how we manage our shots. Whether the ball went where we wanted it to or not often influences how we feel and too often determines how we hit the next shot. Starting and finishing every shot is <u>key</u>! Finishing the shot includes finishing our emotional response. We are <u>not</u> <u>allowed</u> to start the next shot until the previous shot is emotionally complete. This means that we don't walk up to the next tee or onto the green until the previous shot is completely processed.

There are at least two sources of feedback that come from every shot - information and emotion. Information is feedback that is used to make future decisions that allow us to refine the motion. It is used to guide the muscles to perform under a variety of conditions. In terms of emotions, it is important to use our emotions. Whatever comes to us is our source of energy for the next act.

Energy follows intention and emotions are the source of energy to accomplish the intention. If we fight our emotions, or if we continually manage them, our focus of attention is not on putting the ball in the hole! Our focus is in a place that is less than optimal for performance. If instead we channel our emotions into the energy of accomplishment, the next shot can be awesome! This may sound confusing, in one sense we are attempting to make every shot separate and unique, and in another sense we are using what we learned and felt from the previous shot to perform the next shot. In reality, this is true. Our system improves by using what we gained from the previous shot, both information and emotion. However, the next shot must be clearly unique with a clear start and finish of its own. Once again, "this is the one and only time I will hit this ball, under these conditions, in this state of mind, and I will fit the pieces of the puzzle together the best way possible to perform the task." "Reacting" to what just happened is not the same as "responding." Responding is making good choices to perform in a state of mind that will create GREAT shots. This ultimately can lead to GREAT performance!

Golf: Energy in Motion

Emotions are not bad! They are the source of energy we use to play the game. Golf is a game that will draw out every emotion we have, to the extreme. It is our ability to use our emotions that will influence our state of mind and thus, the outcome of play. Everything is stored better in long term memory with emotion. This is why we can remember every detail about very good and sometimes very negative events from the past. They were stored with strong emotion. Thus, it is important for us to store our good shots with strong emotion for future use, and it is important for us to "disown" our negative shots that we consciously "choose not to own."

Anchoring is a common technique used to store good shots. A small gesture, a smile, a thumbs up, etc. will allow us to keep that GREAT shot. On the other hand, this is also a technique that will store the negative shots, with one exception. If the intention of a gesture following a negative shot is to get rid of it and choose not to own it, then the gesture teaches the system to let go of it! For example, if we tap our club on the ground following a negative shot that

> Anchor good shots and anchor letting go of negative shots

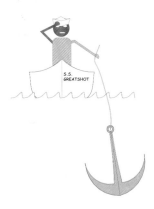

5.5.
GREATSHOT

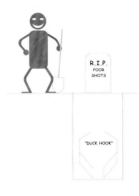

we choose not to own, and see ourselves bury the shot 6 ft under and leave it there, then we teach ourselves to let go of it! What we anchor is letting go! Interestingly, after awhile we no longer need to tap the ground. Our system simply learns to let go of it! I prefer to have golfers do something physical to get the shot away from them, and thus, not own it.

In the early 1980s we conducted a study to assess the emotional responses of twelve LPGA tour players during competition (Crews & Boutcher, 1986). We hypothesized that the better players would be more neutral in their response to shots since the literature at the time was suggesting this approach. This is not what we found! The better players were showing more positive responses. The poorer performers, on this day and according to the money list, showed more negative emotion. Thus, a neutral state was not associated with better golf performance.

Golf: Energy in Motion

Playing in the wind provides a good example of adaptability on the golf course. In many sports wind is a factor that tends to have a strong influence on performance. It affects decisions, balance, state of mind, the swing, the ball and the target. Too often it negatively affects the score. However, someone always manages to play well in the wind and score. Wind is simply one more factor to enter into the equation of play. Whether it is present or not, it always enters into the equation so we simply make sure we are grounded and adapt. If we give the wind strong negative emotion, it is not being used in a way to facilitate our game. It is taking away from our game.

The wind actually has the ability to help us focus, make better decisions, and do many things that work in our favor. The other common tendency I observe is that players often give their ball to the wind. We plan the path of our shot for 200 yards and then we give it to the wind to take into the green. This is going a little too far! While wind influences, especially the tail end of the shot, it is important to plan the interaction with the wind very specifically (the ball will fade in 20 yards to a defined area of the green, land, roll, and stop on the left side of the pin). This is different from just letting the wind take it in—Too Scary!

The system's job is to adapt. It will adapt to any clubs we provide. Fitting clubs to the body can reduce one adaptation for the system and will result in improved performance. Energy will transfer through the system and club to the ball and target more efficiently.

The ability to be adaptable goes along with having a strong ego. Some players choose to display their ego and other players do not display it. Either approach works as long as you have a strong ego inside. The research suggests that the best performers are high in both task and ego goal orientation (Nicholls, 1989). This means that they are motivated to perform the task well, and they are motivated to protect their ego. What is behind a strong ego is good intentions and a strong belief system that supports who we want to be and how we want to play! Our ego, our intentions, and our belief system will allow us to be adaptable! We will further discuss beliefs in Chapter 13.

Last but not least, we can learn a lot from baseball. "Three strikes and you're out!" I once watched a college player miss 11 putts in a row on the low side of the hole. I finally asked, "Are you going to miss the next one on the low side of the hole?" The player responded "No," and the ball missed on the high side of the hole. I often find that golfers use the strategy of forcing the shot.

Three strikes and you are out!

Golf: Energy in Motion

We want to plow through and eventually "what I am doing" will work.

Three times is a charm" or "three strikes and you are out." We have all seen the ball fly to the right, the next one goes left, and the third one travels down the middle. The system can figure it out many times, but not all the time. Especially if we are interfering. However, if the <u>same</u> response has occurred three times in a row, change what you are doing! What you are doing isn't working! Do something different! <u>Be adaptable!</u>

Story Window

Players of the "game of the game" of golf find interesting ways to release poor shots. One player from North Carolina used to touch his opponent's golf bag to get rid of the poor shot. Another player would touch the tree as he walked out of the woods and left the poor shot behind. Anything golfers can do to physically eliminate the shot and choose not to own it will improve performance.

Golf: Energy in Motion

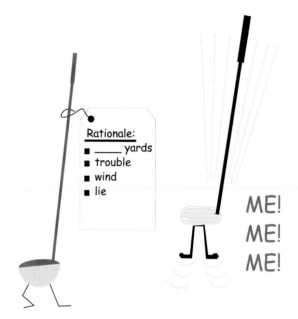

Choices

A very important aspect of adaptability is to know that we always have choices. We may not always be able to control the circumstances and events around us, but we can choose how we wish to respond to the happenings in our lives. Responding is different from reacting! In open skill sports (the ball is moving), we learn to react! However, golf is simply not an open skill sport; it is a closed-skill sport (the ball is stationary). Thus, we respond, not react. We also respond to the target at both a conscious and a subconscious level. Due to the fact that we have ample time in golf, it is better that we choose what we want to do with our time rather than simply react or get it over with quickly! Reacting is a strategy that may work for a short time, but it is a short term fix! While reacting is primarily a subconscious action, responding is both conscious and subconscious.

Let's take for example choosing a club. The conscious takes into account distance, wind, pin placement, possible trouble, etc. Then it decides on the shot to hit, the target, the swing to use, etc.. For example, if everything from conscious logic tells us to hit a 7 iron on this par 3, but we get over the ball and keep hearing 8 iron, which one do we hit? Always the 8 iron! The body and the subconscious swing the club, while the

Golf: Energy in Motion

conscious stays in a good place. If the conscious is swinging the club, we are nowhere near our potential!

I like to use the game of basketball as an analogy for how the game of golf is played successfully, and for how we make choices. In basketball there is a coach and a team. Both have very important roles. The coach is responsible for preparing the team, teaching skills, strategizing, motivating the team, and especially for calling time out. The team, on the other hand, is responsible for learning the skills, thinking on the spot, creating successful motion, and scoring. Interestingly, the coach is not allowed on the court in basketball, and it is the same in golf.

The coach in golf is the mind, or consciousness. It has all of those same responsibilities as the coach in basketball, but it does not swing the club. Remember, the coach is not allowed on the court in basketball! If the mind swings the club, we are nowhere near our capability. The team in golf is the body, the club, the ball, and the target. It is the only team we have so we must learn to play with our team. If there is any member of the team that is not working out today, (i.e., club) substitute the member, at least for the day. They will be fine again tomorrow! The team is responsible for swinging the club and taking the ball down the fairway. The team has access to knowledge the coach may not know, since the coach is not allowed on the court. Therefore, it is important for the coach to listen to the team.

Coach = Mind
Team = Body,
Club, Ball and
Target

Club selection is another good example of the interaction between the coach and the team. The team is swinging the club, so no matter what the coach says, the team always makes the final decision on club selection. The team has input on the type of shot to hit, the strategy, etc. However, at times the team gets a little out of whack (i.e., nervous, anxious, scared) and starts to over-respond to the situation. At these times the coach needs to step in and let the team know that everything is under control and that "this is the plan!" This analogy can be used at any time on the golf course to sort out who is in charge and the best choices to be made. It is very important to know if the conscious or the subconscious is in charge and to give them the responsibility. In reality, we want the conscious and the subconscious on the same team working together. The coach can't play the game for the team. We must instill in the team the belief that they can play successfully and win!

**Time Out!
Be an Observer!**

Often times the team is not able to identify their choices. We are so "into" the game that we can't see the forest for the trees. Taking time out, being an observer, and checking in with the coach are ways to see choices. The team plays very intensely in the game and then steps out to observe and make sure things are going according to the master plan. Unless of course, the player is in the zone. In the zone state, the player simply performs and most everything else is automatic. The coach and the team become one.

Making good choices requires the observer to be able to define what choices exist. A good example is the unplayable lie. We have three options that we consider with an unplayable lie, and then we choose the best one for this particular situation. We actually have the option to do this on every shot. I encourage golfers to play like this ~~this~~ for 9 holes to help them think outside of the box,

especially the tee box! We do not have to hit
driver, iron, putt, putt on every hole. Using
different shots and picking different clubs is
often to our advantage to help us focus
optimally. The body's job is to conserve
energy at all possible times. It must be as
efficient and effective as possible, since it
never knows what is coming. Therefore, the
easy shot in the middle of the fairway with no
trouble around the green often lowers our
intensity of focus, and then we miss the shot.
On the other hand, a trouble shot requires us
to plan the shot well, to image the shot, and to
focus intensely. Expectations are lowered, or
better yet, nonexistent. Planning tends to be
more specific, which is good, and we often hit
a very good shot. Doing all these same steps
on every shot (i.e., ask for more on the easy
shot) would improve our performance for
every shot.

Lastly, we have a choice about how we
respond to events and shots on the golf
course. While we may have a pattern of
reacting to specific shots that have plagued
us for years, we still have a choice about
continuing those patterns. If we choose to
respond differently, we can implement a plan
to do so. It will require awareness, focus, and
intensity to change this behavior. It will
progress slowly to a place where we control
the response rather than the reaction
controlling us.

Golf: Energy in Motion

Story Window

My own experience in putting was an eye opener for me. Putting was not my strength, and it took me a long time to define my putting preshot routine. I felt great when I took three looks at the hole. It was secure and comfortable! After testing two versus three looks at the hole numerous times, I realized I made more putts when I looked two times. At that point I had a choice to make. Do I want to feel comfortable and secure or do I want to put balls in the hole? I chose the hole!

Golf: Energy in Motion

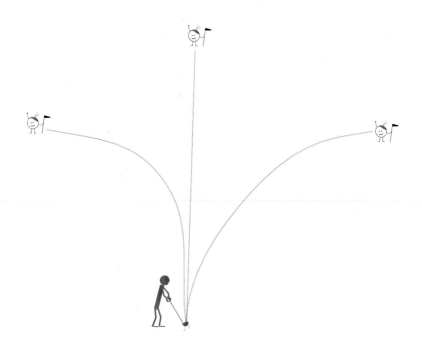

I Know

I know what I am doing! I know why I am doing it! I know that I can do it! This is called "confidence!" When we walk up to the first tee, and prepare to hit, how do we know which shot is coming out? We have one very well-practiced shot that goes straight. We have one very well-practiced shot that goes right. We have one very well-practiced shot that goes left. They are all stored in the system, but we don't often know before the shot which one is coming out. All we can do is create a state of mind that allows the chosen shot to appear.

I conducted a study of the Swedish European Tour Players in the mid-1990s (Crews, Lutz, Nilsson, & Marriott, (1999). The players were instructed to tell us after they putt each 13 ft putt, whether they had that good feeling that they knew the ball was going in the hole, before they putt it. All of these made putts were marked and were analyzed together. The brain showed a quiet, harmonic state. All the processing was complete right before they started the motion. This was compared to 13 ft putts that all went in the hole, but they did not have the "I know" feeling before they started the motion. It is clear that there was more activity, quite well synchronized, on the made putts compared with the confident putts. However, they were not completely done processing, and they did

Golf: Energy in Motion

not reach the harmonic state of optimal performance apparent in the confident putts.

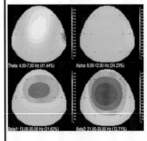 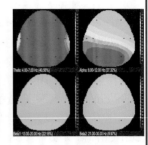

"I Know!" Made Putts   No "I Know" Made Putts

"Anxiety," as we have mentioned previously, is fear of the unknown. Typical unknowns in golf include not knowing where the ball is going, not knowing what swing is coming out, not knowing how I will score today, etc. These are all legitimate unknowns that can cause anxiety and fear.

If confidence is a state of "I know," then it is possible on any given day to determine an "I know." On a GREAT day, I know that the ball is going in the hole, or to my target, and life is great. On a good day I may know with reasonable confidence where the ball is going and that my swing will be close to what I chose. Now on some not so good days, it may be that I only know that I can breathe today. Continuing to breathe may be sufficient and all that we focus on for the day. This information refers to the golfer's state of

Breathe!

mind over the ball. Now what about between shots?

I often find that players, even professionals, do not have a problem-solving strategy for when things aren't going so well. They don't have a plan as to what to check first, second, third, etc. Every error has a physical (mechanical) and psychological (mental and emotional) component to it. If we can define what these are and determine an order of priority for checking them, we can service ourselves effectively. Of the two components, physical and psychological, the physical one is probably the easiest one to fix. If we have a physical (mechanical) problem and know the solution, use it. However, in meaningful games and during competition, it is probably not the physical component that is causing the problem. The physical component is simply a result of the psychological state. Therefore, if we know our psychological tendencies and the physical or mechanical manifestation of that tendency, we can develop strategies to solve the psychological issues before we hit the ball. This in turn will affect the mechanics of the swing, and ultimately, performance.

Thought precedes motion!

Thought precedes motion! It is very important to work backwards to the root of the motion if attending to mechanics is not solving the issue. If the issue is emotional or cognitive, then these areas need to be addressed. It will be very difficult to think correctly mentally if our emotions are not in place. Therefore, the first step is to channel our emotions into an intention that can contribute to solving the problem. Emotions are the source of energy for change. Take "time out" to channel the emotions. Then we have a chance to think clearly, define an intention, and then plan a strategy to achieve this intention. Lastly, we choose a focus that will absorb our thoughts and allow us to subconsciously create the desired motion. The desired motion then creates the shot and allows us to score! Often times the player likes to include a mechanical thought. This is fine if the player is in a receiving state. Sometimes the mechanical thought is not necessarily guiding the motion. It may simply be giving the conscious brain something to think about, to keep it in a good place, while the subconscious swings the club. This way the conscious is in a receiving state (feeling for the motion) and does not interfere while the subconscious swings the club.

While "I know" is confidence, there is a small portion of "I don't know" that is extremely valuable to the game. This small piece of unknown is what creates the excitement, the focus, the challenge, the determination, and the will power to create unbelievable shots. It focuses our attention and guides us to master physical skills that we never dreamed we could perform. Without the small portion of "I don't know," it would not be an experience that could offer so much enjoyment, reward, and fulfillment. We must appreciate the "I don't know" as much as the "I know." This is a game of possibilities!

Appreciate the "I don't know"

When learning a motor skill we move along a continuum from a state of "I don't know" to "I know." This continuum is defined by Fitts and Posner (1967) as three stages of learning.

Analytic   Associative   Automatic

The first stage is the Analytic Stage when we spend a large portion of our attentional capacity sending information to the muscles. Anytime we learn a new motion we recruit many more muscles than we need. As we learn, we refine and become more efficient and effective, and use only the muscles needed to create the motion. This same process occurs in the brain first. We are using many more areas of the brain than we need in the analytic stage. Then as we learn we use only the necessary parts of the brain (Landers, et al., 1994).

As we move along the continuum to the second stage, the Associative Stage, we begin to understand cause and effect—or association. "If I swing this way– I get this outcome– and it feels like this." It is at this stage that we can practice quite effectively on our own.

Golf: Energy in Motion

The final stage is the Automatic Stage. This would be the "I know" stage. It is primarily the subconscious that is creating the motion. However, the conscious must be in a good place in order for the subconscious to create the motion. The question is—"Once we reach the Automatic Stage, do we stay there?" As we all know, some days are more automatic than others. Thus, "I know" is stronger on some days than others. The important decision is to play with what we have for the day. To answer the question, the swing is still in automatic, but changes that occur in us and in our environment tend to alter our performance. Also, there are times we choose to change a component of the swing. For this small adjustment (not the whole swing), we go back to the Analytic Stage. Our goal is to move to the Associative and then to the Automatic Stage as quickly as possible so our focus of attention can be on performance.

The best predictor of future performance is past performance (Williams, 2001). If past performance is not desirable, we must use other sources of confidence. If we only look to the ball to tell us we are good, we are in trouble. The ball can certainly tell us what works for us (i.e., which putter to use, which swing thought works, etc), but it can't tell us what kind of player we are. We must tell the little white ball how life is going to be!

So what are the other sources of confidence available to us? There are many sources of confidence—things that we know we can do:

Breathing

Routines

Finish the swing

Preparation

Treasure box of GREAT past shots

Some players use the terms confidence and comfortable synonymously. However, they are not the same. A player can be confident and not comfortable, or comfortable and not confident. Of the two variables, confidence is the more desirable state. If we are comfortable, we may not move from the level we are playing. We often have to get uncomfortable to change. It's okay! We can still choose to be confident.

Story Window

One of the players from the Arizona State University Women's golf team had a consistent 11 s routine. However, how she spent the 11 s would change. When she was playing well she spent 8 s behind the ball and 3 s completing the routine. When she was not playing well, it was the reverse. The "I Know" was established behind the ball, and the energy flowed from there.

Golf: Energy in Motion

Control the Dial

The state of mind that works on the golf course is one in which we have the perception of being in control. We control the dial! On the outside it may not look like we are in control, but on the inside we know we can perform the task. I have had golfers in my lab whose legs shook for 40 putts straight and they continued to putt ball after ball in the hole. Legs can shake, hands can shake, your heart can be pounding out of your chest, and you can perform awesome shots. It is simply activation and lots of it. With all that energy, the system can be very creative.

A problem arises only when we start putting negative labels on the activation (i.e., "I never do well when I am like this," "I can't do it," etc.). The labels convince the system that we perform poorly under these conditions. Perhaps in the past we have performed poorly in this state, but this does not have to be the current pattern. This highly activated state is actually close to exceptional performance in which we can create unbelievably GREAT shots. It is our negative labels that change this highly aroused state into anxiety. Therefore, it is our labels that can change this highly aroused state back into unbelievably GREAT performance. If we have the perception of

Golf: Energy in Motion

Perceived control allows us to give up the need to control.

being in control, then we can give up the need to control and let the team create the motion. If we never perceive we have control, it is difficult to give the job to the team, and we swing from our head. Not a GREAT place to be!

The state of mind that does not work well on the golf course is "wish and hope." A strong, positive emotional state will allow for clear thinking and conviction. Regardless of the story that is going on around us (albeit a true story), we can create our own state of being and focus on the task at hand. The task is always to get the ball in the hole or to the target. The story may change, our emotions may change, our state of being may be challenged, but the task at hand does not change. Therefore, if we can stay clear about the task and be in a state to facilitate the task, we have a great opportunity for successful performance. Easy to say, not so easy to do!

A common example of this is walking on a balance beam. If the balance beam is 1 ft off the floor, no problem. If the beam is 3 ft off the floor, still a done deal. If the beam is 6 ft off the floor, it may take some concentration and creative self-talk to complete the task. If the beam is stretched between two skyscrapers with a super highway below, emotions would be clearly channeled and thoughts would be carefully focused. The focus would not be on falling and all the possible negative consequences, but on the goal to get to the other side. A strategy would have to be put into place, strong enough to fill all of our attentional capacity so negative thinking and self-doubt could not get in, and we would need guts and willpower to complete the task. My guess is that focusing on mechanics would not be the answer. It would be like a piano player who focuses on their fingers. When a pianist plays 18 notes/s and begins to focus on their fingers, they will not be successful (Proctor & Dutta, 1995). Focusing on the feel (coming from our feet) and the target (the end of the beam) would probably work. Focusing on rhythm, timing, balance with a positive attitude would probably work. It takes guts to focus on target and feel to play golf. Focusing on mechanics is the easier way to play golf; unfortunately, it will get us nowhere near our potential.

So what does "control the dial" mean? First, it means we get to select the station we want to listen to and enjoy. Once we have selected the station, we may need to fine tune it. Reduce the noise in the system. When we have the station clearly defined, we can regulate the intensity or loudness of the information. Higher intensity in the brain usually is more successful for achieving the desired outcome. We do this by turning up the

Golf: Energy in Motion

dial. Too often players decide to TRY to hold onto and maintain what they have (score), and they end up losing the station (and the score).

"Newness" can help change patterns in the brain.

> I conducted a study to examine the effects of a new putter on brain activity (Crews, Lutz, Nilsson, & Marriott, 1999). Interestingly, activity went up in 26 of 32 measures in the brain compared to baseline (putting with their own putter). It seems that it is important for activity to increase, to change the current brain pattern. Then as we habituate to the new stimulus the activity goes down, and we have a chance to establish new brain patterns to improve performance. Using a new club, a new cue, etc., has the ability to change patterns in the brain. While I am not promoting changing clubs daily, when we have negative emotion associated with a club, it is probably a good idea to change the club (at least temporarily) if we want to score.

Under pressure the added adrenaline can change perceptions, our ability to think, and our ability to feel. Often our routine will get faster or slower, and then the timing of our swing gets off. Performance may be less than desirable or better than we could have imagined. However, if we are a strong competitor, this state of heightened arousal is why we play the game. Social golfers also find themselves in this state when the performance is meaningful to them. The <u>key</u> is to <u>use</u> the extra energy or <u>park it</u>!

If it is overwhelming, we can simply park it until after we hit the shot (Bull, Albinson & Shambrook, 1996). There are trash cans on every tee just waiting for us. However, learning to channel it can create unbelievable shots. To do this we synchronize the activity in the brain. It can be very high, but if it is synchronized we will perform GREAT! Thus, controlling the dial is not necessarily turning down the volume. It is finely tuning in the stronger station!

Use it! or Park it!

ERROR PARKING

VALET PARKING

FEAR

SADNESS

FRUSTRATION

This golfer had to sink a 5 ft putt for $300. She was told that she had to pay $100 if she missed (although she wouldn't really have to pay). Her heart rate for this putt was 138 beats per minute, while her regular heart rate was in the 70s. She made the putt and said it was in before it got to the hole. Her brain was highly active, but beautifully synchronized. This is the key!

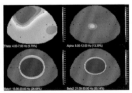

High Synchronous Brain Activity for Final Successful Putt

Golf: Energy in Motion

Story Window

Several years ago a player from the LPGA was looking to improve her scores. Most of her game was in good condition. However, she left almost every putt short. It didn't bother her to leave putts short. She had a hard time watching them roll past the hole. Her subconscious was well trained to prefer short putts. The goal was to convince the subconscious that it was preferable to leave putts long rather than short if they weren't going in the hole. For every putt that passed the hole she would say, "I'd rather be that much long than short." However, this was still not getting them past the hole. To get her activation state up we imaged being in the gym, the state she used right before she lifted weights. This did it! When she created this energy state, the balls went in or past the hole!

One of our ASU collegiate players became anxious as soon as she stepped onto a putting green. Her blinking rate, an indication of anxiety, would double! We decided to "park" the anxiety before she walked onto the green and focus on the routine. Instead of nine looks at the hole before she putted, we reduced to two looks, and the balls began dropping in the hole. Putting and scores improved tremendously!

Golf: Energy in Motion

Magic Box

Every player must have a magic box, or whatever we choose to call it, on the golf course. When things are going well, we simply play and enjoy every minute of it. However, when things aren't going so well we must have resources. These resources we store in our magic box.

I envision that a tool kit is used for fixing swings on the golf course. In the tool kit we might have screw drivers to direct the swing, pliers to tighten and loosen the muscles, drills to remember what we are suppose to be doing, hammers to hit the ball when swings aren't working, vices to hold everything in place, etc. As you remember there is a physical and psychological component to every error. When something goes wrong, we get out our tool box and start looking for something to fix. However, we often find that we are missing just the tool we need. This is because it is not the physical component that is causing the problem. To manage the psychological component, we resort to our magic box. The more important the game, the more likely we will be using our magic box instead of our tool kit.

The magic box will have a variety of resources to choose from depending on the state we are in and the circumstances surrounding us. We will know which resource to use to optimize performance in each situation. Over time, patterns emerge that guide us in our magic box selection. For example, when I am feeling anxious, a certain swing usually comes out. Therefore, I will focus on a special thought to make sure I put the ball in the fairway.

The magic box will contain breathing, imagery, self-talk, beliefs, past great shots, a preshot routine, a post shot routine, starting and finishing, motion, birds singing, nature, houses, food, movies, songs, etc. Let's discuss these resources in greater detail.

Breathing is magic! The routine is <u>started</u> with a big breath that says "Clear out the miscellaneous. We are going to focus!" The <u>second</u> important breath is right before we start the motion. It is important to let all of our air out and then swing. When we have no air, we will have no tension, but more importantly, we will be centered and settled.

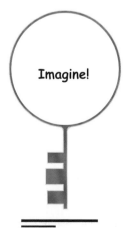

Imagine!

Imagine what you want! Imagery is one of the most powerful resources we have. It may be visual (see), auditory (hear), kinesthetic (feel), olfactory (smell), gustatory (taste), or intuitive (sixth sense). Using all of the above is what creates the best performance. Once again, if we can image it we have a great chance of performing it. On the other hand, if we can't image it, pick a different shot. It is not likely to happen.

The voice in our head can be very influential. Be sure we know who is talking and what they are really saying. We do not have to listen to everything we hear going on up there. There are at least two voices and probably more. It is important to decide who is giving us valuable and reliable information and who is giving us a hard time. STOP! TIME OUT! Switch the channel if necessary. We do not have to be a victim on the golf course. In addition, there are clearly words to eliminate on the golf course (listed below). Each of us may be able to add a few of our own. Also listed below are the replacement words to use on the golf course, and we can add a few to the list as we hear our own patterns.

Words to Eliminate	Replacements
1. Don't	Do_____
2. Can't	Do_____
3. Have to	Do_____
4. Need to	Do_____
5. Should	Do_____
6. Try	Do_____
7. Just	Do_____

All of us have a bank of past GREAT shots. We remember them well because they were stored with great emotion. Some of them were probably hero shots, some of them well planned, prepared created shots, etc. We can call up these shots from long term memory anytime we choose. They will create positive emotion and confidence in our ability to perform.

The Magic of Being Done!

A preshot routine brings consistency, perceived control, concentration, organization, and preparation to the motion. It provides a means for us to complete each step of our preparation and clearly be "Done" with each step of our preparation. It is the "Magic of Being Done" that lets us swing. The routine is where the pieces of the puzzle are put together to set us up for optimal performance. When we are not in a good place or are very nervous, we can always focus on the components of the routine, and they will get us through. Routines help us feel consistent, confident, and they will fill our head with thoughts that will keep us in a good place to perform successfully

The post shot routine helps us manage the aftermath of the shot. In order for us to stay in control of the dial, a routine trains the psychophysiological system to respond appropriately. After the shot it is as simple as 1. release, 2. quick analysis, and 3. "It's history" if we don't like it, and "It's the future" if we do like it. Either way "It's Done!"

Clearly starting and finishing the motion insures that we are consciously present at the beginning of the swing and that we stay consciously present until the motion is complete. Fear often causes us to bale on the shot. Breathing out before we start the motion helps us to be present and settled, and finishing the shot maintains conscious awareness. This way, the subconscious is free to perform the motion without interference from the conscious.

Motion is magic! When fear sets in we often freeze. Keep moving and use a rhythm or pace to your motion. The body knows where it is when it is in motion. It gets lost sometimes when it is still.

Birds singing, nature, and houses surrounding the golf course are ways to focus our attention between shots that will keep us in a neutral-to-positive state of mind. They enhance a receiving state which is optimal for the golf course.

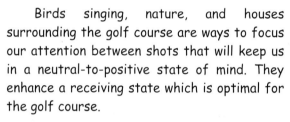

Food, movies, and songs are also techniques to keep our consciousness in a neutral-to-positive state of mind between shots. These thoughts have the ability to fill our attentional capacity with thoughts that often elicit strong positive emotions.

Keep a neutral to positive state of mind.

There are many more items that can go in our magic box. In fact, some of them can hang on our golf bag. For example, pictures of our dog or someone we think well of, verses or affirmations that remind us of who and how we want to be on the golf course, and lastly, happy faces or stars to reward ourselves for GREAT accomplishments.

Golf: Energy in Motion

Story Window

One of the best imagery stories I ever heard came from a junior golfer, of course! When she was 5 years old she used to think that there were little people inside the golf ball with steering wheels. She would tell the little people where to go to get in the hole. On the days the ball didn't drop, she figured out that they weren't listening to her!

Life cereal was a life saver for an ex-tour player. Every time the anxiety would come before a shot, she would simply think of her favorite cereal "Life" and hit the shot. Interestingly, life would be better and the ball would fly!

Golf: Energy in Motion

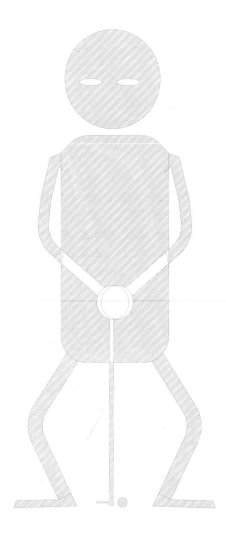

Believe

According to Merriam-Webster (1994), beliefs do not need proof of existence. These are statements that we choose. They are more than just thoughts. Once we choose the beliefs, our energy and the energy around us moves towards these desired outcomes. Therefore, we put into motion everything available to achieve the belief. We become aware of the resources around us that will help us achieve our belief. It is very important to have a set of beliefs about ourselves and our golf game. Most players have a set of beliefs in place about their golf game, even though they may not define them as beliefs. It is also important to have beliefs about ourselves. I believe there are some beliefs that are important for all golfers to have in order to optimize performance. I will list a few of them:

Beliefs do not need proof of existence.

1. I am a GREAT putter! Since 47% of the game is putting, it is very important to have the belief that I am a great putter. If we have putt well during one round of golf, then we were a GREAT putter during that round. We simply want to increase the frequency of that successful putting performance.

2. I am GREAT from _____ yards and in! We can select the yardage as 100 yards and in, 50 yards and in, etc. It would be advantageous to see ourselves as having a GREAT short game since 67% of what we do is short game. The yardage we select can get longer as we continue to improve.

3. I fly out of the blocks! This means that when we walk onto the first tee and are ready to hit, we are ready to sprint. We cannot wait to hit the first shot or play the first hole to find out what kind of day it is going to be. That needed to be done on the practice range. Warming up our muscles is part of getting ready. Finding out what game we are playing with today is the other part of getting ready on the range. If today is a fade on the range, we play a fade. If today is our "B" game instead of our "A" game, we make decisions accordingly. If we are under-reading or over-reading putts because of the speed of the greens, we adjust. Now we are ready to score!

4. The last 3 holes are my Best! When we arrive at 16 tee it is like we start over. No matter what the day has been, we have the belief that we will play the last 3 holes as the best holes of the day. We finish strong, we sprint in, we run through the finish line (not to it). More tournaments are won and lost on the last 3 holes. When we have this belief, we will pace the first 15 holes and look forward to the last 3 holes. This way we can win the tournament, the match, and beat the course!

5. **I am adaptable!** I can adapt to anything that comes to me today! We have spent a whole chapter on this concept, but it is a very important belief for us to have to score well.

6. **I control the dial!** This means that I call the shots. I regulate the intensity. I am in charge. We have also devoted a chapter to this important belief.

7. **I coach the team!** I synchronize all the variables that contribute to my success. I set the stage for optimal performance. I stay with the team throughout the motion. I plan the strategies that work today and in the future.

Last, but certainly not least—

I Believe in Me!

Golf: Energy in Motion

There are also beliefs that we adopt that do not help us synchronize our energy for success. These beliefs cause anxiety, fear, and block the energy paths in our system. Let me list some examples with alternatives:

1. I should make every putt from 3 ft in.

Or, 3 ft putts and less are missed every day on all the tours. For every 3 ft putt I miss, I will make a long putt!

2. The golf course is groomed to give me good lies and good bounces.

Or, the course is designed to challenge me. For every shot it takes away, it will give me one back!

3. I should leave myself an uphill putt.

Or, get the ball past the hole on the high side and leave yourself a tap in!

4. Duck hooks are from being overly aggressive.

If I believe, I do not need patience!

Or, duck hooks can be from being tentative and pulling everything in close to my body due to fear.

5. If I'm just patient, good results will come.

Or, if I believe, good results will come.

6. If I miss this birdie putt, it's okay, I will still have my par.

Or, every shot counts equally, par is not an option!

7. If my long game is on, my short game is off. If my woods are on, my irons are off, etc.

Or, we choose to be on for every shot and off between shots!

Each golfer can define their own beliefs about their game. It is important to say them, to write them, and to review them daily. These beliefs direct all of our decisions and energy about where we are now and where we are going. Our beliefs help formulate our attitude. "Attitude is everything" on the golf course and in life. It is more often attitude that putts the ball in the hole!

"Patience!" A common phrase in golf is "if I am just patient..." I often wonder, "What are you waiting for?" If you believe, you don't need patience. If you believe you simply stay active, strategic, moving forward, and learn from every step of the way!

Our beliefs define the glasses we use to look at the game of golf. It is very important that we choose and define the glasses for each and every day. They strongly influence everything we see, hear, feel, and how our system responds to events of the day! I personally like rose-colored glasses!

Choose your glasses!

Golf: Energy in Motion

References

Adler, C.H., Crews, D.J., Hentz, J.G., Smith, A.M., & Caviness, J.N. (2005). Abnormal co-contraction in yips-affected but not unaffected golfers: Evidence for focal dystonia. *Neurology, 64*, 1813.

Anderson, L., & Crews, D. (2001, March). Golf science prize winner. *Golf Magazine*, 94-96.

Bargh, J.A., & Chartrand, T.L. (1999). The unbearable automaticity of being. *American Psychologist, 54*(7), 462-479.

Bull, S.J., Albinson, J.G., & Shambrook, C.J. (1996). *The mental game plan*. Brighton, UK: Fotodirect Ltd.

Crews, D.J. (1994). Research based golf: From the laboratory to the course. In A.J. Cochran & M.R. Farrally, *Science and Golf II* (pp. 127-137). London: E & FN Spon.

Crews, D.J., & Boutcher, S.H. (1986). An exploratory observational behavior analysis of professional golfers during competition. *Journal of Sport Behavior, 9*, 51-58.

Crews, D.J., & Landers, D.M. (1993). Electroencephalographic measures of attentional patterns prior to the golf putt. *Medicine and Science in Sport and Exercise, 25*(1), 116-126.

Golf: Energy in Motion

Crews, D.J., Lutz, R., Nilsson, P., & Marriott, L. (1999). Psychophysiological indicators of confidence and habituation during golf putting. In M.R. Farrally & A.J. Cochran (Eds.), *Science and Golf III* (pp. 158-165). London: Human Kinetics.

Crews, D.J., Martin, J., Hart, E.A., & Piparo, A.J. (1991). *The effects of EEG biofeedback, relaxation, and imagery training on golf putting performance.* Paper presented at the North American Society for the Psychology of Sport and Physical Activity, Asilomar, CA.

Csikszentmihalyi, M. (1990). *Flow: The psychology of optimal experience.* New York: Harper & Row.

Easterbrook, J.A. (1959). The effect of emotion on cue utilization and the organization of behavior. *Psychological Review, 66,* 183-201.

Ellis, A., & Dryden, W. (1987). *The practice of rational emotive therapy.* New York: Springer.

Feist, J. (1985). *Theories of personality.* NewYork: CBS College Publishing.

Fitts, P.M., & Posner, M.I. (1967). *Human performance.* Belmont, CA: Brooks/Cole.

Hawkins, D.R. (2002). *Power vs. force.* Carlsbad, CA: Hay House.

References

Landers, D.M., Han, M., Salazar, W., Petruzzello, S.J., Kubitz, K.A., & Gannon, T.L. (1994). Effect of learning on electroencephalographic and electrocardiographic patterns in novice archers. *International Journal of Sport Psychology, 22,* 56-71.

Merriam-Webster, Inc. (1994). *Merriam-Webster's dictionary of English usage.* Springfield, MA: Merriam-Webster.

Milton, J. (2003). Poise and noise. *The University of Chicago Magazine, 95*(4).

Molander, B., & Backman, L. (1989). Age differences in heart rate patterns during concentration in a precision sport: Implication for attentional functioning. *Journal of Gerontology, 44*(3), 80-87.

Nicholls, J. (1989). *The competitive ethos and democratic education.* Cambridge, MA: Harvard University Press.

Piparo, A.J., Crews, D.J., & Hart, E.A. (1991). *Level of fitness and performance of a precision task.* Paper presented at the Sport and Exercise Psychology Symposium, College Park, MD.

Proctor, R.W., & Dutta, A. (1995). *Skill acquisition and human performance.* Thousand Oaks, CA: Sage Publications.

Schmidt, R.A. (1988). *Motor control and learning: A behavioral emphasis* (2nd ed.). Champaign, IL: Human Kinetics.

Singer, R., Lidor, R., & Cauraugh, J. (1993). To be aware or not aware? What to think about while learning and performing a motor skill. *The Sport Psychologist, 7,* 19-30.

Smith, A.M., Adler, C.H., Crews, D., Wharen, R.E., Laskowski, E.R., Barnes, K., Bell, C.V., Pelz, D., Brennan, J.S., Sorenson, M.C., & Kaufman, K.R. The "Yips" in golf: A continuum between a focal dystonia and choking. *Sports Medicine, 33*(1), 13-31.

Stelmach, G., Crews, D.J., Martin, P., & Cheetham, P. (1998). *The influence of age and skill on variability of movement during the golf putt.* Paper presented at the Third World Scientific Congress of Golf, St. Andrews, Scotland.

Thomas, K.T., & Thomas, J.R. (1994). Developing expertise in sport: The relation of knowledge and performance. *International Journal of Sport Psychology, 25,* 295-312.

Toole, E. (1999). *The power of now.* Novato, CA: New World Library.

Williams, J.M. (2001). *Applied sport psychology* (4th ed.). Mountain View, CA: Mayfield Publishing.

APPENDIX A

Golf Awareness Inventory

Your Swing

Do you have trouble getting started?

Do you get stuck?

Do you follow through?

Do you finish?

Do you tend to push it or pull it?

Do you lose your balance at the end?

Do you over-swing?

Do you come over-the-top?

Do you complete your back swing?

Do you get faster, slower, or go the same speed?

Do you focus on going back or going forward?

Do you get done with it?

Do you get hurt easily?

Your Ball

Do you tend to dig in or barely catch it?

Do you tee it high?

Do you hit it high or low? Right or left?

APPENDIX A (continued)

Does how it fly determine how you feel?

Do you get bad bounces?

Do you talk to your ball?

Does it listen?

<u>**Your Routine**</u>

Do you breathe?

Do you image?

Do you look where you are going?

Do you use a practice swing on full swings?

Do you check and recheck aim?

Do you regrip?

Do you move your feet?

Do you get fast or slow in pressure?

Do you set the club behind the ball or slide it in behind the ball?

Do you do it the same every time?

APPENDIX A (continued)

<u>Your Game</u>

Do you play fast or slow?

Do you socialize or focus? Is it the same when things go well? When things don't go well?

Do you warm up?

Do you always know the score? Everyone else's too?

Do you depend on your caddy or do it yourself?

Do you have distance gaps in your clubs?

Do you get penalty shots?

Do you try new things or stick with what you know?

Do you value "how it looks" or "where it ends up?"

Do you like playing with people better than you, the same, or lower skilled?

Do you play better or worse in trouble?

Do you play better or worse when you get angry? (Not frustrated)

(Please see the next page for further instructions!)

APPENDIX A (continued)

Please read through the answers to your questions and reference the answers to LIFE instead of to golf. Some responses may apply and some may not. ENJOY!